NORIGAMI

The Art of Norwegian Paper-Folding
By John Roth, M. A. N.*

*Master of Arts, Norigami

Thanks to all whose love, laughter, and expertise helped give birth to Norigami, especially Paula, Gordon and Geri, Diane Gummeson, Sharon Betcher, Kathy Pususta, M.K., Kate, and Raff Fynn, Veryl Johnston, Cindy Litlabø, Mandy Ylvisaker (now, THAT'S Norwegian!), The choir at Reformation, Patty Wagner, Vicki Patschke, Allan Mahnke, Mike and Else Sevig, and Larry Stark.

©1991 Adventure Publications, Box 269, Cambridge, MN 55008

Cover design and illustrations by John and Paula Roth.

ISBN: 0-934860-77-7
Printed on recycled paper

Lovingly dedicated to
Justin and Spencer and to the
daily unfolding of
their wonderful lives

Special Thanks to

Marji (a "St. Ole") Mike Shirley & 303
YOUR NAME HERE

For Buying this Book

SEE NEXT PAGE
FOR DIRECTIONS

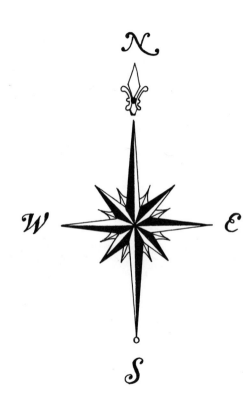

WELCOME TO THE FOLD

To those who call "Norwegian Art" a contradiction in terms, or go around joking that Scandinavians would never take the time to fold anything they couldn't eat, it may come as a shock that there exists a splendid Norwegian art of paper-folding, known as "Norigami."

Readers who are familiar with "origami" will perhaps wonder whether Norigami is a derivative or transplanted version of the Japanese art. No way, Axel...

The Oriental version is famous for its grace, tenderness, and purity. Norigami, on the other hand, is down-to-earth and practical. Instead of paper cranes, pretty fish, and elegant flowers, Norigamists make paper "lefse," "snow", and "lutefisk helper."

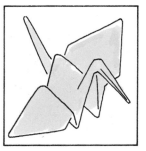

JAPANESE CLASSIC:
" CRANE "

NORWEGIAN CLASSIC:
" SNOWBALL "

WHAT TO USE

Way down dere in the back of the book are scads of special Norigami paper to cut out and fold. Or you can use lefse (see p. 26) or any other paper you've been saving for no good reason. (See examples below.)

JUNK MAIL

ENVELOPES

NEWSPAPERS

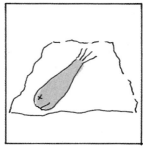

FISH WRAP

AERIAL VIEW OF NORTH DAKOTA IN JANUARY

1. PLACE SHEET OF WHITE PAPER ON TABLE   2. VIEW

SNOWBALL

PAPER SNOWBALL   GUARANTEED   FUN WHEN THROWN   AT NEAREST SWEDE

NORWEGIAN JUGGLING

KEY TO DIAGRAMS

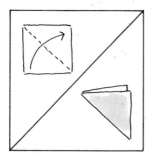

BASIC FOLD (RESULT)

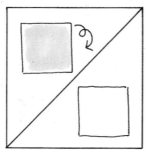

INVERT PROJECT

USE TAPE

MAKE COFFEE

PRETTY FUNNY NORIGAMI JOKE #1

14

FOOD

LEFSE

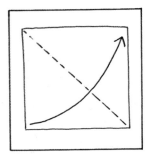 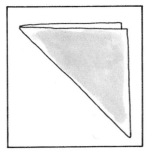  

PAPER LEFSE'S　　BIG APPEAL　　LOOKS AND TASTES　As GOOD AS REAL

LUTEFISK HELPER

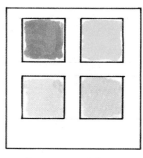

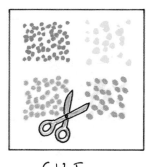

CHOOSE PAPER   CUT   TOSS   SERVE

FORTUNE LEFSE

ROLLING PIN

   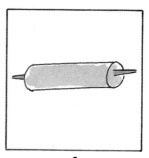

PAPER, TOOTHPICK   SPOT OF GLUE   ROLL AND TAPE IT   "VAER SÅ GOD" *

* PRON. "VAR SHA GOO"
NORWEGIAN FOR
"THERE YOU HAVE IT!"

BREAD PUDDING

GLORIFIED RICE

SCALLOPED POTATOES

CREAMED HERRING

NORWEGIAN FOOD QUIZ

KRUMKAKE

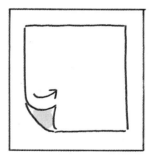 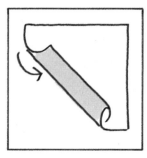  

CURL FROM CORNER   CAREFULLY   SERVE WITH COFFEE   MILK OR TEA

NORWEGIAN POWER LUNCH

SHAKERS

MOVERS

HIGH ROLLERS

FLATBREAD

A LITTLE PAPER   AND "PUNCH"   MAKES A DANDY   FLAT LUNCH

NORWEGIAN BIRTHDAY CAKE

NORWEGIAN CAKE

CHEAP BUT ARTY

MAKES YOU "LEIF" OF ANY PARTY

ANONYMITY BAR

CUT TWO STRIPS   ROMANTIC LIASON   UFF DA-THE <u>PASTOR</u>!   THAT VUSS CLOSE

LEFSE-GAMI

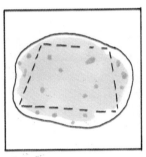

CUT A SQUARE

SEE DIRECTIONS ON PAGE 55

SEE PAGES 54-56

WEAR OR EAT

VIKING-HAT

LEFSE-GAMI:
THE ART OF
NORWEGIAN FOOD-FOLDING

Long before lefse was eaten, it was worn. In the beginning, Thor created Ole and Lena, placed them in The Fjord of Eden, and admonished them not to eat anything hot or spicy.

Then came "The Fall," followed closely by "The Winter," so cold and snowy. Lefse was made into britches, and worn inside the fig leaves, providing warmth and comfort.

Soon, creative folding of the lefse into imaginative undergarments became an artistic pastime. (The classic "triangle" shape has survived in modern-day lefse.)

When "The Spring" finally came, a few of the fanciest designs were set aside, and the rest of the stuff was eaten.

Today, "Lefsegami" is practiced mainly by a weird Lappish cult, but is enjoying a modest comeback amongst folklorists.

LEFSE HOME WEATHER STATION

LEFSE HOME
WEATHER STATION

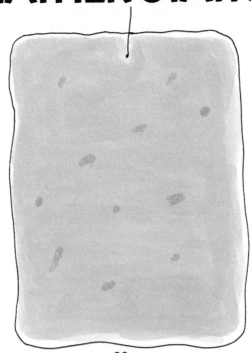

1. ATTACH
LEFSE TO
STRING

2. HANG
OUTSIDE
WINDOW

3. MONITOR
CONDITIONS
USING CHARTS
ON FOLLOWING
PAGES :

Lefse Home Weather Station Guide:
WIND

NO WIND

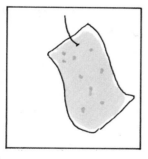

YOOST A LITTLE WINDY

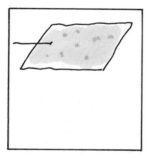

PRETTY WINDY

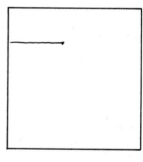

TORNADO

Lefse Home Weather Station Guide:
TEMPERATURE

FILL

SATURATE

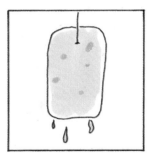

32°F OR ABOVE

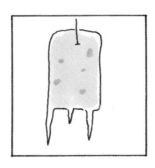

32°F OR BELOW

Lefse Home Weather Station Guide:
PRECIPITATION

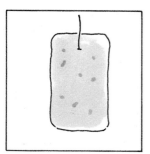

NO RAIN

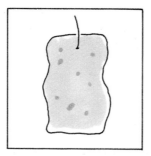

WARPED: HUMID

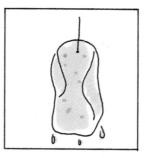

RAIN

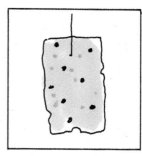

HAIL

TROUBLESHOOTING TIPS FOR WEATHER-STATION USERS

LEFSE HANGS
BELOW WINDOW:
<u>STRING</u>
IS <u>TOO LONG</u>

USER HAS
MISUNDERSTOOD
DIRECTION #2
ON PAGE 30

LEFSE NOT
VISIBLE:
<u>WASH WINDOW</u>

LEFSE TURNS
BLACK:
<u>POLLUTION</u>—
<u>MOVE TO COUNTRY</u>

WINTER

SNOW

DECORATE YOUR STUDIO WITH DRIFTS OF NORIGAMI SNOW

SNOWBLOWER

SNOWY TABLE   NO PROBLEM: CLEAN IS YOOST   A PUFF AWAY

CROSS-COUNTRY SKIS

CUT 2 SKIS

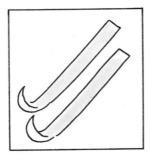

CURL THE ENDS

TOOTHPICKS
AND
"WAGON WHEELS"

FUN WITH
FRIENDS

JUL LOG

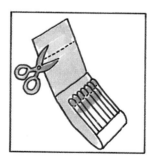

CUT OFF 1 INCH

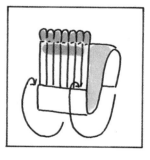

CURL AND TUCK

REMOVE ALL
BUT 4 "CANDLES"

GOD JUL !

TOBOGGAN

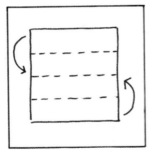   

FOLD AND CURL   YOOST LIKE SO   MOUNT ON   "NORIGAMI SNOW"

SNOW SHOVEL

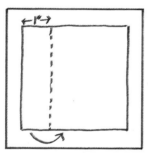

FOLD

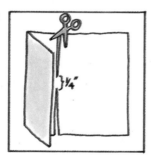

LEAVE ¼ INCH
IN CENTER

CURL TIGHTLY

CURL AROUND
FIRST CURL

42

SNOW SHOVEL

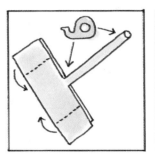

TAPE HANDLE,
FOLD BLADE

TAPE BLADE

CURL BLADE

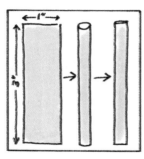

CUT, CURL,
FLATTEN HANDLE

SNOW SHOVEL

BEND TO
FORM HANDLE

INSERT

PERFECT FOR

NORIGAMI SNOW

THE
NORWEGIAN
"O"-TESTER

NORWEGIAN "O"

Norwegian speech delights the ear with its rich assortment of unique textures and sound-colors. Chief amongst these, however, must be the Norwegian "O". Now, for the first time, non-natives wishing to develop an authentic Norwegian "O" can use the Norigami "O-Tester." Cut it out, and follow the directions to a Norwegian "O" that will be the envy of all who hear it.

YOUR NORWEGIAN O-TESTER

Cut on dotted line.
Roll to form cylinder.
Size your "O" on page 49.
Place cylinder in mouth.

Use test phrase:
"The Oslo snow is only so-so."

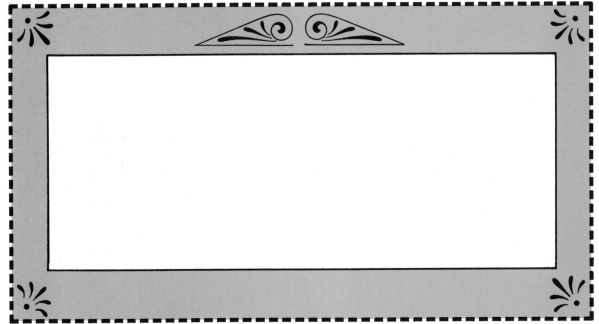

SIZING YOUR O-TESTER

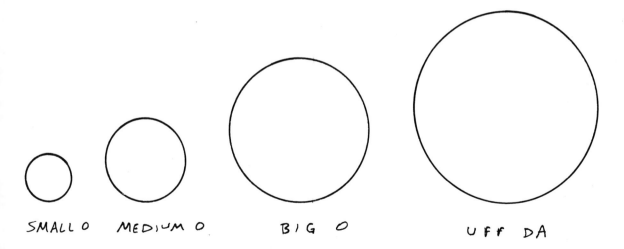

SMALL O   MEDIUM O   BIG O   UFF DA

AUTOGRAPHS OF REAL NORWEGIANS I HAVE MET

VIKINGS

VIKING SHIP

CUT AS SHOWN

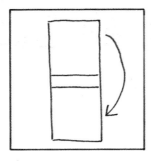

FOLD IN HALF

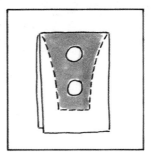

CUT ON DOTTED
LINE AND PUNCH
TWO HOLES

CLIP

VIKING SHIP

CAREFULLY
REMOVE ALL
BUT THE TEN
MATCHES IN-
DICATED IN
FOLLOWING
SQUARE:

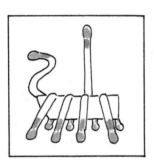

BEND MATCHES
AS SHOWN

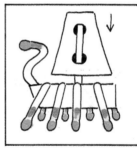

RIG SAIL

ON THE FJORD

VIKING HELMET

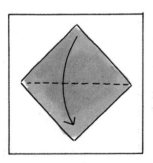

NORIGAMI
PAPER SQUARE

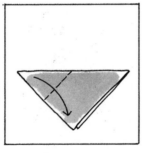

LEFT SIDE

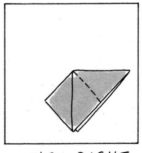

THEN RIGHT

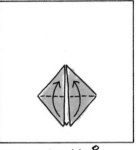

FOLD UP
TOP LAYERS
ONLY.

VIKING HELMET

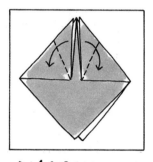

DIAGRAM NOW
ENLARGED

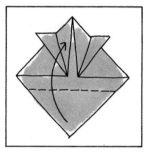

FOLD UP TOP
LAYER ONLY

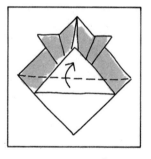

FOLD UP
DOUBLE LAYER

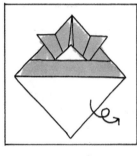

INVERT

55

VIKING HELMET

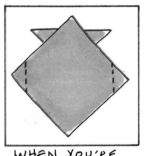

WHEN YOU'RE
DONE

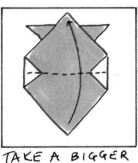

TAKE A BIGGER
SQUARE

TURN THE PAGE

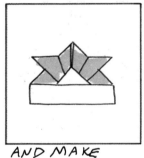

AND MAKE
ONE TO WEAR...

VIKING HELMET
YOU CAN WEAR

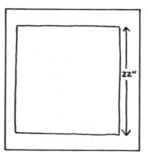

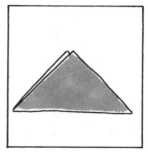

BE THE APPLE   OF HIS EYE   IN "VIKING   THIS SYTTENDEMAI!
                                             WEAR"

57

NORWEGIAN GLITTER

STORE-BOUGHT GLITTER

(KINDA PRICEY)

NORWEGIAN VERSION

CHEAP— BUT SPICY

KENSINGTON RUNESTONE

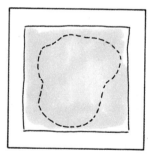  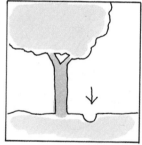 

CUT OUT

INVENT MESSAGE

BURY IN FIELD

UNCOVER AND TOUCH OFF SCHOLARLY DEBATE

STILL ANOTHER PRETTY FUNNY NORIGAMI JOKE

HOUSEHOLD
NORIGAMI

MOIST TOWELETTES

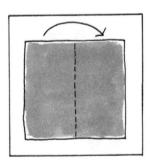 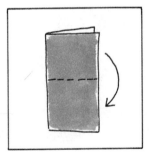  

BUDGET BABY-WIPES

 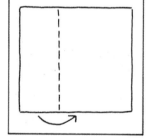 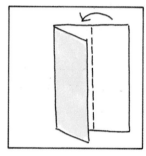 

NORIGAMI WIPES   DO JUST FINE   WHEN "SAVINGS" IS   THE BOTTOM LINE

TOILET PAPER

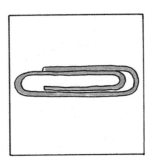

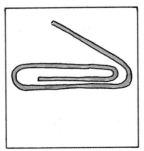

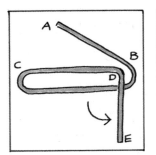

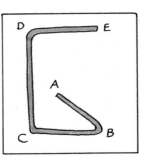

PAPER CLIP SHOWN FLAT ON TABLE

BEND

"ABC" STAY ON TABLE. GRASP "DE" AND BEND UP AT "C" TO FORM...

STAND

TOILET PAPER

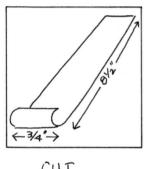

CUT

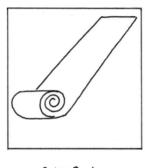

CURL

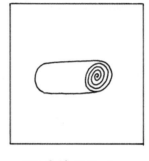

TIGHTEN

NICE FOR
NORWEGIAN
DOLLHOUSE

NORIGAMI FREQUENT FOLDER CARD

THIS CERTIFIES THAT

_____

**IS A FREQUENT FOLDER
ENJOYING THE LIFE-ENRICHING
BENEFITS OF**

NORIGAMI

"The Art of Norwegian Paper-Folding"

SPORTS, TRAVEL,

AND SEX

NORWEGIAN MINIATURE GOLF

CUT AND CURL FLAT PIECE TO MAKE BAG

CLIP HEAD FROM ONE MATCH AND BEND INTO HANDLE

CLUBS

MATCH-HEAD MAKES A NICE GOLF BALL

NORWEGIAN TRIATHALON

LUTEFISK EVENT

MANURE PILE
POLE VAULT

"NORWEGIAN O"
COMPETITION

GO FOR THE
GOLD

MAP OF THE BLACK FOREST

YOU CAN FOOL
SOME OF THE
PEOPLE

SOME OF
THE TIME

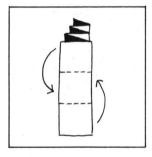

BUT YOU CAN
ALWAYS FOOL

A GERMAN

PAPERHENGE

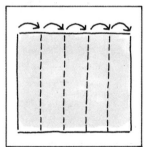

ACTUAL SIZE:
MAKE ABOUT 10

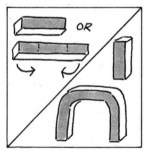

FOLD SOME AS
SHOWN

POSITION

WAIT FOR DRUIDS

NORWEGIAN MEN'S MOVEMENT

HARDANGER RETREATS

ICE FISHING

CRYING IS O.K.

"MEN'S BOOKS"

NORWEGIAN SEX MANUAL

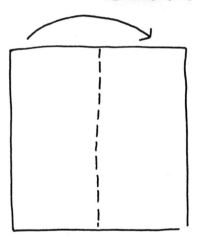

1. FOLD

2. PRESENT TO FRIEND

GREAT (BUT THIN) NORWEGIAN CLASSICS

GRADUATE
LEVEL
NORIGAMI

TIMELINE:
THE EVOLUTION OF
PAPER-FOLDING

B.C. 1491
MOSES FAILS
AT STONE
FOLDING

B.C. 1140
SAMSON'S
INNOVATIVE
"TEMPLE-FOLD"

LATER ON:
VIKING FINDS
PAPYRUS FRUS-
TRATING

A.D. 105
TSAI LUN
INVENTS PAPER,
SETS STAGE
FOR NORIGAMI

NORIGAMI: RIGHT-BRAIN OR LEFT-BRAIN?

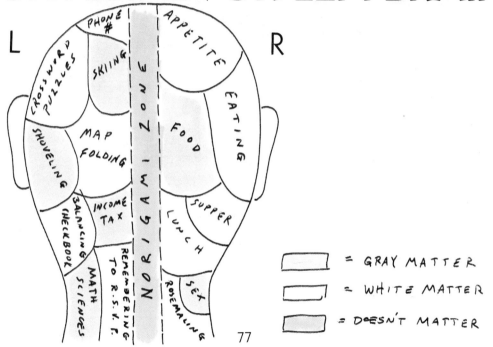

L   R

PHONE #
APPETITE
CROSSWORD PUZZLES
SKIING
EATING
SHOVELING
MAP FOLDING
FOOD
NORIGAMI ZONE
BALANCING CHECKBOOK
INCOME TAX
SUPPER
LUNCH
MATH SCIENCES
REMEMBERING TO R.S.V.P.
SEX
ROSEMALING

= GRAY MATTER

= WHITE MATTER

= DOESN'T MATTER

77

MICROGAMI

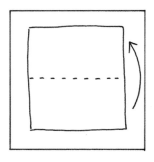 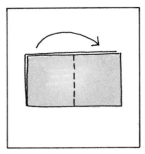 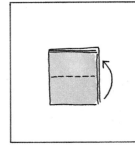 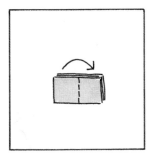

MICROGAMI

  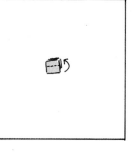 

MICROGAMI

NORIGAMI PLANETARIUM

ASSEMBLE TOOLS

PUNCH OUT THE CONSTELLATION CARDS ON PAGES 82 – 87

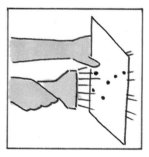

PRACTICE ON WALL OR CEILING

LIGHTS OUT!

PLANETARIUM
CARD #1

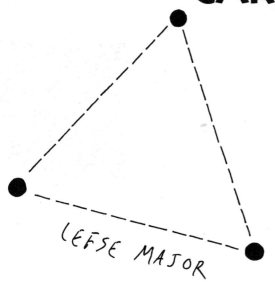

LEFSE MAJOR

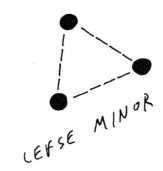

LEFSE MINOR

PLANETARIUM
CARD #2

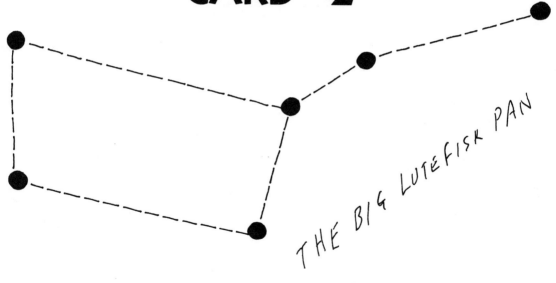

THE BIG LUTEFISK PAN

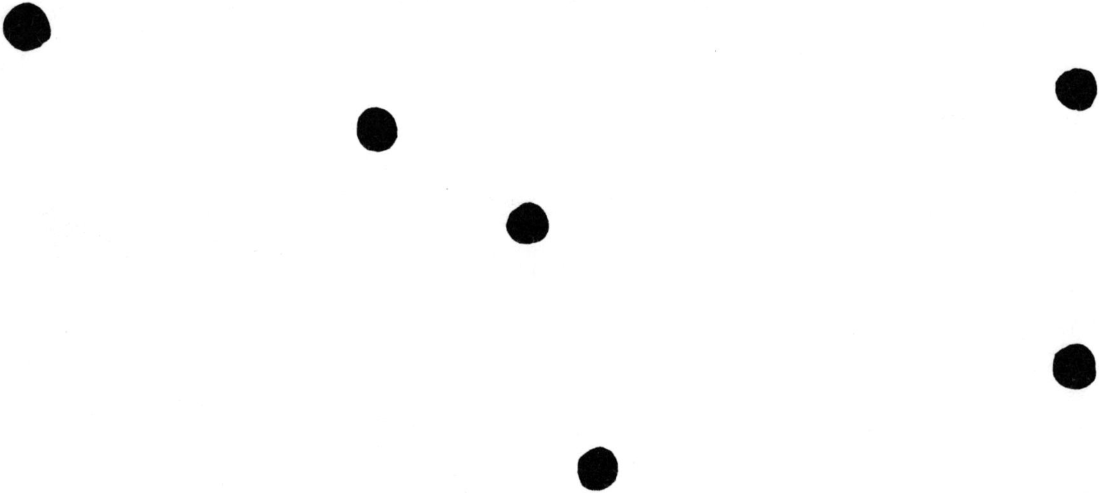

PLANETARIUM
CARD #3

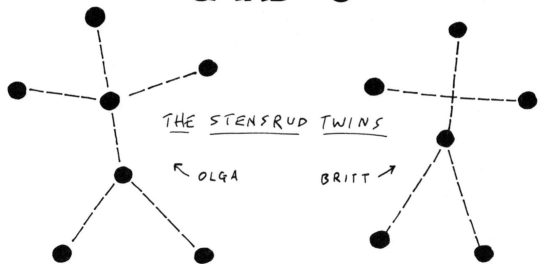

THE STENSRUD TWINS

↖ OLGA   BRITT ↗

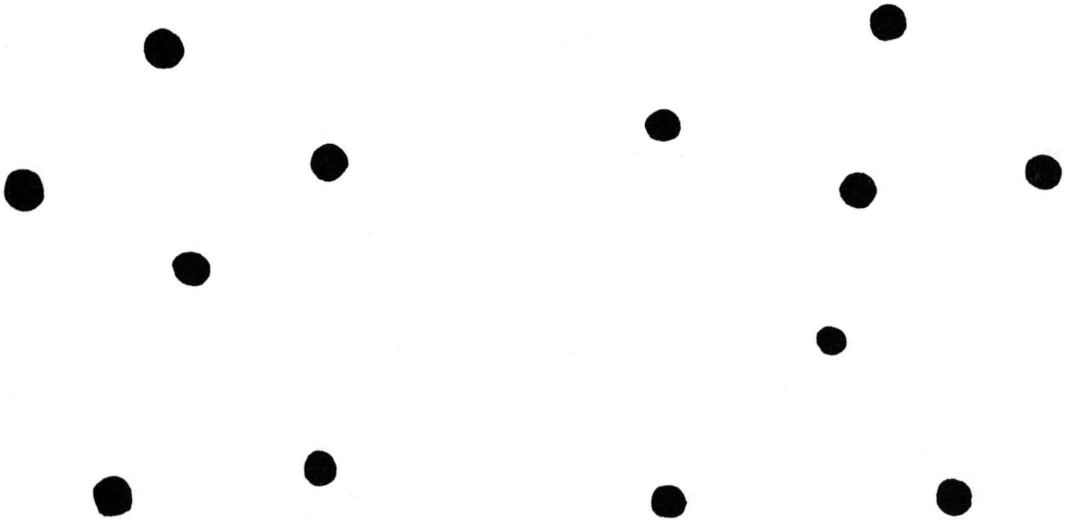

PLANETARIUM
CARD #4

PASTOR TORGRIMSON'S CHAIR

NORIGAMI
FOLDING
PAPER

CUT HERE

CUT HERE

CUT HERE

CUT HERE

CUT HERE

CUT HERE

CUT HERE

CUT HERE

CUT HERE

CUT HERE

CUT HERE

CUT HERE

CUT HERE

CUT HERE

CUT HERE

CUT HERE